Woulda, Coulda, Shoulda... Didn't

How I almost filmed in all 50 States in 1 year.

by
Jayon O. Mckinney
better known as
King Spencer

01 DALLAS

TEXAS JANUARY 1, 2017

I was stuck in the middle on whether or not this was a good idea. It was the end of December 2016 and I accepted a project offer from Zie OKC to film a project in Dallas, Texas. I'm definitely not a fan of driving out of state, especially considering the fact I didn't have a car. But I really appreciate and respect Zie as a person, so I did what was necessary to make it work. I called up my cousin, T. Reed, and asked him if I could pay him a few bucks to give me a ride to Norman, Oklahoma and as usual, he came through in the clutch and helped me out.

When I finally arrived to Norman I hopped out, grabbed my belongings and prepared myself for a 3 and a half hour drive to Dallas, Texas. Thankfully Zie was using a truck for this trip because my legs tend to cramp up in small cars when I take long 1 hour or longer trips. One of the disadvantages of being 6'5. I have been a "yes" man for a fair amount of my career as a freelance videographer and it has landed me in many situations that I would wish I had not experienced. But in addition, being a "yes" man has exposed me to many situations that has made me the man I am today, and for that I am proud.

We spent the majority of December 31st filming for Zie's project and the majority of the night editing what we shot. I have always been commended for my speedy turn around and this night was no different. Zie and the others at the house decided to go out to bring the New Year in. I on the other hand didn't really have much interest in going out, being that I don't smoke nor drink, and mostly introverted, the club and party scenes aren't much of a vibe for me.

I wasn't aware of the self-perpetuated adventure I was about to experience once the clock struck 12. I ended up going to bed around 11pm and cracked open a book, The Art of War by Sun Tzu.

It was 12am when I heard the regular booms and pows that notified the world that the New Year had arrived. I can vividly recall my emotions at that moment. I was bothered, I was angry, I was sad. I felt like a complete failure. Another year had passed and here I was lying in bed. I was still charging the same prices for videos, I wasn't a legitimized business, I didn't own a car, I was still living with my parents and had a much longer list of disappointments that I'd rather not get into. I was ashamed of myself.

It was in that moment that I decided there would never be another year that passed me by where I couldn't rejoice at some phenomenal personal success that I had accomplished within my God blessed 12 months. In this same instance, I thought to myself what my first major personal success of 2017 would be. Immediately I realized I was in Texas; I had a shoot set up in Oklahoma the following day and I would be in California a week later. "I'm going to every state in America this year", I thought to myself jokingly, but deep down inside I knew this was it. I read in a book that it was in your favor to make your goals and milestones public, because people will usually hold you accountable for the things you promised. I put this into practice on January 1st, 2017 while on the way back to Oklahoma from Dallas, Texas.

We pulled over to a gas station just outside the city of Dallas to fill the gas tank and grab refreshments. I hopped out of the truck and asked Zie if it were cool if I sat on top of the bed of the truck so he could take a picture of me. He told me to stand on it. With no hesitation I jumped on top of the bed of the truck, grabbed myself with my ashy hands, bit my Honduran souvenir necklace, tossed up three fingers and smirked my lips. My adventure across the country started right here.

02 OKLAHOMA CITY

OKLAHOMA JANUARY 2, 2017

On the second day of 2017, I was in Oklahoma City just after leaving Texas. This gave me extreme confidence because I had already finished one state and was instantly in another, two for two. A small success, nonetheless, very appreciated because I already had a flight to California booked. This massive weight of success was parading upon my soul, I could just see myself passing the finish line of 50 states within my deadline. I could see how everyone would be so proud of me and I would have endless blog interviews over my trip and famous people wanting to meet me because they were so inspired by what I would soon succeed at. Although this hallucination would be far from the reality of my success, it felt really good and inspiring to bathe in.

Day 2, in Oklahoma City I had a video shoot for a song named Chucks and Cortezs with my good friend Marvaluzz Thug of Ruthless Records. I was thankful to have T. Reed with me because I didn't have a car, and he came in handy a lot of the time and he didn't charge me an arm and a leg. Oklahoma City was a fast and easy trip, and I was ready to get home because I had already been in Texas for so long. After we finished the Chucks and Cortezs music video, I put my drone in the sky and captured a picture of myself in front of the city's skyline as best I could at the given angle. Only my second day and already 4% of my journey was complete.

03 LOS ANGELES

CALIFORNIA JANUARY 10, 2017

During my 365-day mission to reach every state in one year, I probably visited California 9 or 10 times. My first visit to California was to Los Angeles in May 2015. Every year I would visit LA once or twice a month on my own dime, so it's fair to say I was pretty well established as a videographer amongst several communities. My next visit to California in 2017 was on January 10th. Once I landed, I headed straight to The Marathon Store on the corner of Crenshaw and Slauson and my good friend J. Stone let me use his discount to buy a Crenshaw t-shirt half off. I walked outside the store and asked him to take a picture of me at the storefront. This was my third state in less than two weeks. I was happy but this state was easy, because I had been there so many times before.

I want to skip to mid-2017 to another, more special visit I made to Los Angeles, California during my expedition. The time I shot a music video with Nipsey Hussle. I have met the great Neighborhood Nip on many occasions between trips to LA and projects in other states. I feel it's important that I tell the story of the very first time I met Nipsey Hussle to display the magnitude of influence this artist and idealist had on my life. The first time I met Nipsey Hussle was at his studio in Burbank on May 18th, 2015. It was also the first time I had ever been to Los Angeles, so this was a surreal experience for me.

I started listening to his music about 5 years prior to this visit when he released his mixtape called The Marathon and he was my favorite artist since. I was filming a video for J. Stone of All Money In and we were wrapping up the shoot getting a few more shots at the All Money In studio. J. Stone hosted me on many of my trips to Los Angeles and made sure I was safe and sheltered, for the most part. I was a big fan of J. Stone through his music with Nipsey Hussle so just being in his presence was a little unbelievable for me being that I'm from a small city in Oklahoma where you rarely hear about people being around celebrities as casually as I was.

Someone had brought pizza to the studio and told everyone present they were welcomed to take a piece if they desired. As hungry as I was, I didn't mind grabbing a slice so I sat my camera down and headed toward the box of pizza right outside the room on a table in the hallway. No sooner than I could get into my first step I see a tall, light skinned, tattoo-faced man with a white and green Celtics branded letterman jacket on. I knew exactly who this person was, but I felt like my eyes were deceiving me because it could not be possible that this person was walking right in front of me. I wanted to say something, but I had to remind myself that this person did not know me and I didn't want to come off rude.

All of a sudden, my hands started sweating, I began to feel extremely nervous and very anxious. This feeling I am describing is called "star-struck". It sounds crazy when you hear that people pass out when they meet some celebrities but I understood, in full, the possibility of that happening after seeing Nipsey Hussle that day. Nipsey walked pass me into a room at the end of the hallway and I played it smooth as if I belonged there, grabbed a slice of pizza and returned to my chair, all while trying to tame my composure. The night progressed and Fatts came into the room and told me my Uber ride had arrived, helped me pack my belongings and walked me out to the car. Just as he was about to close the door, he said a few words and finally asked me, "did you get to meet Nip". I wasn't expecting to actually meet Nipsey, but I had a feeling this was soon going to change.

I told Fatts that I hadn't had the chance, so he told me to come back inside. Everything from this moment forward was slow motion. We walked across the street and into the side gate, down the pass way, through the screen door, and up the hallway all one single step at a time. This had to have only been about a 10-yard walk, but it definitely felt this it was 50. Nipsey was already standing there with a cup in his hand speaking with someone, so Fatts and I patiently waited until their conversation was over. As they walked away Nipsey looked at me with a plain look on his face and Fatts approached him and began speaking.

"Nip this the homie Spencer from Oklahoma," mispronouncing Oklahoma. " He came all the way out here to shoot J. Stone's videos," Fatts spoke.

At this point I believe I can hear my heart thumping in my chest or maybe it's the bass from one of the studios in the back of the building, but I wasn't sure. My hands are in my pocket because this was the most logical way to control the perspiration from vomiting out of my palms. After Fatts finished introducing me, Nip nods his head, takes a drink from his cup and steps toward me while reaching for a handshake.

"What's up bro, my name is Nip. I appreciate you for coming out here and for what you're doing for my brother."

I didn't want to shake his hand, but I wiped my palm as hard as I could and as discreetly as possible when removing my hand from my pocket to return his gesture. He didn't budge when our hands connected so I felt a sense of accomplishment. I thought it was very interesting that he introduced himself even though he probably could have guessed that I already knew who he was. All of the built-up anxiety from the moment I saw him walk past the pizza up until I walked back inside the screen door instantly released in the matter of seconds.

I started by saying,

"No problem bro, I've been a fan of your music for a long time. Me and my brother listen to all of your music. You have really changed my life".

Reading this doesn't sound nearly as fan-spoken as it does hearing it. Fatts then asked me if I wanted to take a picture with Nip, then I said I didn't, because this won't be our last time working together, and I was right. It wouldn't be our last time working together and I wanted to reserve as many fan related tendencies because I was actually interested in a real casual and/or business relationship with the All Money In family. August 8th was the day I shot the music video with Nipsey Hussle.

04 PORTLAND

My first day in Portland, Oregon was interesting because I arrived during the same time I was reading a book called "How to Win Friends and Influence People" by Dale Carnegie. Every day I had been reading parts of the book up until this day where I got to exercise some of the ideas that were introduced in that powerful book. When I made it to my hotel at the Crowne Plaza Downtown Portland right across the highway from the Moda Center, I walked in with the intention of learning and remembering the name of every person I met and taking a genuine interest in who they are while staying in Oregon for the next 3 nights. Doing this didn't have any immediate effects on my life, but I can say when I returned to this same hotel two years later, the hotel concierge remembered who I was, where I was from, what my goal was and also hooked me up with some great Blazer tickets.

The weather in Portland, Oregon wasn't the most desirable with snow covering everything the eyes could see, but I appreciated it more than ever because the regularity of trees and familiar architecture made me feel more at home than ever. I went from being in Los Angeles the past few days prior to walking into the hotel in Portland and wouldn't be home for many more days. I filmed with a few artists in the area like Donte Thomas, Bocha, Kid Moe and a lot more, so it was a busy and well-planned week in Portland. I shot most of the videos for little to nothing, but I stemmed great and irreplaceable relationships from some of these experiences. When I was ready to upload a picture of myself in Portland, I wanted to be near a landmark, and to no surprise, like many states to come, it was in front of the basketball arena.

Lucky enough to find a stranger waiting for a bus in front of the center, I was blessed enough to get a picture and not have to chase down a stranger I feared might try and run off with my phone in this land that was foreign to me. In every city I visited I was always paranoid and couldn't help it. I am thankful for this unshakable feeling of paranoia because it always kept me aware of my surroundings. This is necessary when you were in places like the many I would visit and doing things I was doing with strangers. This year I would witness, endure and survive the terrible weather, breathtaking airplane turbulence, gang shootouts, homelessness and eviction that this beautifully cruel world has to offer.

05 VANCOUVER

WASHINGTON JANUARY 19, 2017

Vancouver, Washington was the 5th state I visited in the month of January. Five states in one month really had me feeling hopeful in my endeavors to reach all 50 states. I was in Portland Oregon when my friend Kidd KM told me how close Portland is to the border of Washington. This information made me light up. I instantly began tapping into every resource I had to find artists in the Washington area. Thankfully, Kidd KM knew some artists that were from Vancouver and they were in Portland often. We made one phone call, exchanged contacts and began discussing potentially shooting a video that same night. I was happy to find out that The Dead Phone Dummies were just as willing to get the project done as I was. I recall a member of The Dead Phone Dummies telling me they got their name from going to parties and always noticing that their phones were going dead.

Later that night, one of the artists in their group picked me up from my hotel and we got in route to Vancouver, Washington just over the bridge. It was a little bit of a ride across town but once we finally arrived, I was happy to meet the rest of the crew. We did a few scenes at one of their friend's homes then later moved on to a park where we did some shots next to a lake. Our last shots were at another house where a bunch of girls came by and partied a bit with their crew. When we finally finished filming, we went back to Portland but on the way there we stopped at a gas station to fill up and get refreshments. It was there I noticed a building that had the name Vancouver on it just across the street from where we were. I took this opportunity to get my 5th state photo to share with my followers. I asked one of the Dead Phone Dummies members that I was riding with to take a picture of me at the station.

06 PHOENIX

ARIZONA FEBRUARY 22, 2017

I was in Phoenix, Arizona for only one day, but I made it well worth it. I have a cousin, Dominic, who was staying there at the time, so before I arrived, I was already blessed enough to have living arrangements situated. My first experience I can remember was walking out of the airport with my hoodie on and remembering how hot it was. That day in Phoenix was interesting because during the day, it was a hot desert summer but by nightfall it was really cold outside. My cousin greeted me with open arms when I arrived and so did all of his family. It wasn't long before I was shooting my first video with my friend Shag Loc and he gave me a fair tour of his side of the town.

Later that evening I was able to shoot with a couple more Arizona natives, Paco Doe and Rich Makin Moves. It was cool to meet all of these artists while in the city because they all had different stories and perspectives on the city of Phoenix. I was near the mountains when the sun began to set, and I decided this would be the perfect place to illustrate my location. Here, I had my picture taken of me in my 6th state, within 2 months.

07 CLEVELAND
OHIO FEBRUARY 24, 2017

When it came down to Ohio, I knew I had so many different cities to choose from. Cincinnati had a strong hip-hop scene, but so did Cleveland, Columbus and Dayton. So, when it came down to choosing where I would go, I did like I do in most hard choice scenarios. I went with the cheapest. I was in Phoenix, Arizona when I made this decision and when I was searching prices I found a non-stop one way from Phoenix to Cleveland for only $103. This was a clear-cross the country experience for the same price as a pair of Air Force 1's, and I wasted no time booking it.

When I landed in Cleveland around 7PM at night on the 23rd of February I had no clue what to expect. I was just there. I was able to contact a couple of artists through Instagram, and a good man by the name of Killuh B connected me with an artist who was available in the city. He was the first artist I worked with, St. Clair Bear. He was maybe 10 years older than me but had just as much energy if not more. Bear hosted me for the majority of my stay and was kind enough to show me around the city of Cleveland. We went to a few spots in the hoods of Cleveland and I also got to visit the famous Lake Erie.

It was cool seeing all the American landmarks that I learned about in grade school. Later that night we went downtown by the Rocket Mortgage Fieldhouse where the Cav's play and the city was busy. I saw a large Lebron James billboard on the side of a building and instantly knew I wanted to take my 7th state photo in front of it. Bear grabbed my cell and told me to pose, so I crossed my arms and smirked for what would be my 7th state in 2 months. Hello Ohio!

08 PROVIDENCE

RHODE ISLAND FEBRUARY 26, 2017

I landed in Rhode Island around 2 o'clock on Saturday afternoon. I will never forget how cold it was when I landed. Rhode Island was special because this was the furthest I had ever been away from home without going outside the country and it was my first time visiting New England. Right when I landed, I booked a room with hotwire hot rates and got a room as close to the airport as possible. I was lucky to get a room at the Sheraton Hotel, which is always a great brand to lodge with.

I had been keeping on and off contact with one particular person from Rhode Island named Chachi Carvalho a week or so prior to my visit. I was having a hard time finding artists in Rhode Island by searching hashtags on Instagram, so I googled the phrase, "Rhode Island Hip-hop". Luckily, I was able to find a blog that mentioned a bunch of artists around the state including Chachi. By the time I made it to Rhode Island he was available to meet and welcomed me with open arms.

I went to my hotel room to unpack some of my things then called an Uber so I could go meet Chachi. I was staying in Providence, Rhode Island, but I believe the address I met Chachi at was in Pawtucket. I was a big fan of the show Family Guy and it never occurred to me that Pawtucket was a real city in Rhode Island. This fact made the trip a little more special. I arrived at Chachi's address and he was outside sitting on the steps. The Uber stopped the car so I could get out and right when Chachi saw me I knew I would enjoy my evening. He welcomed me with a hug and invited me into his home. When I entered into his house, he introduced me to all the members of his family and he fed me some delicious spaghetti.

We started shooting the video shortly after my meal, so we went outside to the driveway where his good friend pulled up in a brand-new Beamer. His good friend commended me on my goal to reach every state and wished me success. We shot scenes in the driveway then Chachi and I drove to a park a few miles away to get more scenes. Chachi was full of energy and had very intelligent conversation. He was a dreamer, and he spoke life into the topics we discussed. There was never a dull moment. After we got our scenes at the park, we headed over to a show that was happening at one of the bars. I had no clue that the night life would be so alive, but I soon found out that Providence is a college city. There are 4 colleges in Providence and many more in the surrounding cities so needless to say, downtown was active. Chachi introduced me to a bunch of local artists and we just hung out and enjoyed the scene for the remainder of the night.

The following day I met with another really popular artist by the name of Passionate MC. Chachi set this shoot up for me and I was happy it worked out because I wanted to shoot for as many artists in town as I possibly could during my short visit. Passionate MC was very popular outside of Providence, so it was a really good look once the video we shot was released.

09 SALT LAKE CITY

UTAH FEBRUARY 28, 2017

I arrived in Salt Lake City, Utah late on a Monday night. It was nearly 12AM by the time I made it to my hotel, yet I was still fortunate to find some artists who were willing to work with me at such a late hour. SLC's downtown had the appearance of all the other big cities I had visited, but it was unusually calm, quiet and reserved. There weren't very many cars on the street, monkeys playing at the cross lights, buses, taxis, Ubers or police officers consuming the well-lit streets. But I did remind myself that it was barely midnight. I assumed to myself that SLC, like Tulsa, is a city that sleeps. I was only at my hotel about 30 minutes before Phobia arrived with her minions and we began to shoot our video.

It was a swift and easy process, and they were definitely an interesting group. Phobia today is a really popular artist in LA and has a sound that is unique to all genres and much appreciated by her fan base. The morning following my shoot I visited the stadium where the Utah Jazz play basketball and decided this would be where I documented my 9th state visit. It was always fun to upload the pictures to Facebook and Instagram because I got a rush from the feedback from my followers and it felt good to see myself progressing in the goal I set.

10 ATLANTA
GEORGIA MARCH 12, 2017

Atlanta, Georgia on March 12th was full of surprises. I flew to Atlanta to meet with one of my favorite artists, Yung Scrilla, and as always, he had a pretty big project on his hands. He picked me up from the airport and we hung out around the city. We visited the mall, got a bite to eat, visited his family then did what he likes to call, "rapper shit". We started off by filming our first music video that included Scrilla and Famous Gang. The shoot was simple and to the point. Later that night or very early the next morning rather, Skooly, who one half of the famous rap duo known as the Rich Kids, came through and put a song together with Scrilla. It was cool to share a room with someone who has had as much musical success as Skooly and to witness him working with Scrilla.

We got lots of studio footage and we later filmed a music video. I decided that I would take a picture with him to best illustrate my trip to Atlanta, and also it was the most convenient given the time and our location. After Skooly left we retired for the night and woke up the next morning ready to film more. We ended up shooting two more videos that following morning and rushed to the airport because I had to fly to Las Vegas for another shoot.

11 LAS VEGAS
NEVADA MARCH 13, 2017

Although I had been to Nevada plenty of times in the previous years, I made sure of it that I visited Las Vegas early in my trip. Las Vegas, Nevada has always been one of my favorite cities because when you're on the Strip it has a "big city" feeling. All of the lights, the people, the traffic, street performers, stores galore, there is just a lot going on and I like it. Before I landed in Las Vegas I was in Atlanta, Georgia and I had actually missed my originally booked flight to Las Vegas. I ended up catching a later flight, and this was a sort of a big deal because I was supposed to be in Vegas by a certain time in order to start filming a music video for an LA originated artist by the name of Steven G.

This was our first time working together and I was already setting a bad first impression. It looked like I wasn't even going to make it to Las Vegas, but I was able to make ends meet and show up a few hours late. Steven G had already booked a huge Airbnb in Henderson, Nevada and brought his whole group from LA with him. This shoot had to happen. I arrived in Las Vegas around 8 PM on March 12th and Steven G was already waiting at the airport. Although things started later than we hoped, Steven G was still happy to shoot and we got right to work.

We started by going back to the Airbnb so I could put my things away and meet the rest of the group. It was great to meet the featuring artists Fly DA Uno, Nino Almighty Gold, Geo Brown and the rest of the group. We moved on from the house to the Strip and we just free-styled the shoot throughout the night. We ended up at Caesars Palace and we were in the lobby when I decided I wanted to take my picture to update my followers on my progress. I stood in front of the magnificent fountain and lifted my chin for my 11th state.

12 **DENVER**

COLORADO MARCH 21, 2017

Denver, Colorado was an interesting trip. The days before I flew into Denver I was in Austin, Texas for a very popular music and film festival called South by Southwest (SXSW). My brother Richard dropped me off at the airport early in the morning, around 5AM. My flight took off at 7AM and the airport was crawling with pedestrians. I saw some famous people checking through customs like Method Man and Ty Dolla Sign. The flight wasn't too long, about 2 and a half hours and I was really excited to be in Denver. Not only because it was my first time visiting, but because I was there to shoot some very special videos.

My friend GI Joe from LA was doing a show with Nipsey Hussle and I couldn't be much happier. I'm a big fan of them both but with all the successes the All Money In team had been announcing, I felt like it couldn't have been a better time to be a part of the progress. I caught an Uber straight from the airport to the venue that the guys would be performing at and walked in just in time to preview the performance through sound check. The second I walked in I heard Nipsey Hussle rapping the lyrics to his song over an instrumental to an empty venue. I walked across the middle of the floor as calmly as I could, but inside I was very excited so see Nipsey Hussle doing his thing.

I walked straight onto stage from the left side staircase when I saw GI Joe OMG, Newport, B.A., DJ Double-E and DJ VIP. We all greeted each other and then GI Joe gave me the rundown of what to expect for the rest of the evening. After sound check we left the venue to go to the Double Tree hotel that Nip was staying at. When we arrived Nip and Jorge Peniche were in the lobby feasting. They invited us over for lobster and fettuccini. This was a dream come true for me. Out of state, eating lobster with some of the most prestigious artists from the west side of the country and it was all for free. After we finished eating GI Joe and I started filming his music video.

The next day I booked a room in another part of Denver and prepared myself to shoot a video for a new client, Mathias Medina. Mathias was native to Grand Junction but recently moved to Denver and was hiring me to shoot his first music video. I've always loved to hear I was the first videographer someone had ever worked with because I always feel like I bring a high quality customer service standard to my projects that many videographers are challenged with meeting. When I met Mathias for the first time it was really easy. Mathias is a cool, calm, humble and easy-going person. He introduced me to his family and offered me food to eat.

We shot some footage downtown and moved on to a parking garage that had a nice view of the Denver night skyline. We had just finished doing a drone shot when I realized I had been in Colorado two days and still hadn't taken a photo to show where I was. I handed Mathias my cell phone, sat my camera down on the ground in front of me and turned my face away from the camera. That day I documented my 12th state in only three months. A long way to go, but already, I had made it quite far.

13 MEMPHIS

TENNESSEE MARCH 31, 2017

Tennessee was an interesting trip because I was on this trip working with one of my all-time favorite Tulsa artists. This artist has a chapter in every level of my progression, and I would think its vice versa as well. MDot Benjamin invited me to Tennessee to film not only a music video, but an experience. He would be working with the Memphis native, Richlord and also shooting a music video with another Memphis native and rising artist, Finesse2Times. I wasn't very sure of who these artists were, but like many of the artists MDot introduced me to, they were very popular and one of them was more so infamous.

It was March 30th when we arrived in Tennessee and it was one of my least favorite trips, only because we drove. Tulsa, Oklahoma to Memphis, Tennessee is only about a 6-hour drive but sitting still for 6 hours has never been my preferred way to travel but for MDot I would make that sacrifice. We checked in to a hotel immediately after we arrived and then went to the studio where we would meet Richlord. Richlord wasn't the timeliest person but he did eventually arrive. It was late, but MDot and Richlord recorded a song that night and I documented the whole experience.

When we left the studio, we decided to go to one of Memphis's popular attractions, Beale Street. Beale Street to Memphis is like what Bourbon Street is to NOLA, a street with lots of bars, food and entertainment of all varieties. It was on our way towards Beale Street that we were walking past the FedEx Forum where the Grizzlies play basketball. I felt this was a special landmark to me and decided it was here that I wanted to document my next milestone. Thanks to MDot, I made an extra step in completing my goal. 12 states later I finally arrived at number 13.

14 MINNEAPOLIS

MINNESOTA MAY 7, 2017

The day I landed in Minneapolis, Minnesota was a particularly special day because I was meeting with one of the most inspirational and motivated people that I personally know, Yancey Duckett. Yancey had a somewhat adventurous childhood and has stayed in multiple areas throughout the United States. Thankfully, he stayed in Minnesota at the same time I arrived because thanks to him I had a place to stay and the opportunity to meet a lot of people and make a little extra cash while I was there.

Yancey picked me up from the airport the day I landed and he informed me about the speaking engagement he had coming up the next day. He started a movement called, No Start No Finish, which was in place to encourage people to get started NOW on pursuing their purpose in life. He and his team had been promoting and putting boots on the ground to get as many people as possible to show up and not only support, but also learn at this event. To help the success of the event I used my camera to film some promotional videos for the brand the day I landed.

He had a 13-week challenge going on to help people create good habits and break bad financial habits, so we filmed one video that would serve as the guide for the beginning of each week. Once we finished shooting the 13 week videos, he pointed out to me that the bridge we were on was somewhat monumental to the city of Minneapolis - Lowry Avenue Bridge. It was at this bridge that I decided that I would make my 14th Territory.

15 LITTLE ROCK
ARKANSAS JUNE 11, 2017

June 11th was the beginning of a very important relationship in my short career as a videographer. A week or so before, I received a call from a stranger named Adrian Bradley. Adrian is the soon-to-be husband of Tulsa Legacy Charter School's Executive director, Carlisha Williams. Interesting enough, I met Carlisha Williams while working on a project I was doing for someone else, Ebony Combs, and I met Ebony Combs while doing a project for John McDaniel. Networking is king in a business like videography and it will take you places you could literally never imagine.

But this special relationship between Adrian and I started with him seeing a project I did for Carlisha. At the time Adrian worked for a company called The Marketing Arm, and his job was to travel the US and do promotional events for mainstream companies like AT&T, Cantu, and whatever else clients the company inherited. When he called me, the conversation was short and to the point, "I need a videographer. I can pay you this amount. I need you at this place, at this time". This was very convenient for me because I usually deal with clients that have a load of questions, that aren't very sure what they want, and are not usually that straight forward about paying.

Adrian offered me a handsome amount in comparison to how much I normally charge and compared to how hard I normally work. Again, I called my cousin T. Reed to give me a ride and included his cut for taking me on this trip. Adrian set up our hotel, travel per diem and all the expenses during the visit. While in Arkansas I also filmed music video projects for NHB Lloyd and Phatte400. These two locals welcomed me with open arms, and we shot some videos.

I was able to meet a few other local artists and make some other connections while in the city of Little Rock. It wasn't until T. Reed was driving past the Verizon Arena that I remembered that I needed to take a picture to display that I had visited my 15th state. We pulled over to the side of the street and jumped out the car. I looked over my shoulder, grabbed myself, and tossed up three fingers: one step closer.

16 DETROIT
MICHIGAN JULY 16, 2017

My trip to Detroit was not like most of my other trips for 1 specific reason; I was working with Starz/ AT&T and their hit tv show, Power. I had been working with a company called The Marketing Arm, and they hired me to recap an event that a Detroit local radio station was hosting. This gig would include food, music, and celebrities. The TV show Power was doing a small tour to bring more awareness to the show and also to reward a lot of the loyal watchers. The people on the tour were 3 of the TV shows popular characters, Rotimi, Joseph Sikora and J.R. Ramirez. I didn't know that I would be meeting these guys many more times in the near future, but I was excited to be a part of such a huge project.

My job was easy, all I had to do was record the entrance of the guests, a fan/talent question and answer segment, then a short performance by Rotimi, and finally the meet and greet. I enjoyed this project because it paid well, compared to what I made for music videos, and because it was much simpler to edit.

I reached out to some of the local artists in hopes to shoot a few music videos while in Detroit, but I was unsuccessful, probably because I wasn't trying very hard. I was already satisfied that I filmed for Power and I wasn't crazy about making a bunch of crazy offers to strangers in hopes that they would allow me to shoot for them. I left Detroit the following morning and it wasn't until I was already at the airport that I realized that I hadn't yet uploaded a picture of myself in Detroit. Unfortunately, I couldn't find any landmarks at the airport, so I had to settle for taking a picture in the chair. I had my power shirt on, so it wasn't a completely random photo. So, at the airport, is where I published my 16th achievement of 2017.

17 CHICAGO

ILLINOIS JULY 17, 2017

My trip to Chicago was similar to my Detroit and Houston trips. This is because I was in Chicago to film another gig with Starz hit tv show, Power. The only thing that could have made this better was seeing 50 cent, but unfortunately that wasn't likely. The same thing happened at this gig in Chicago as what happened at the other Power gigs. Q&A, prizes and giveaways, meet and greet and performance from Rotimi. Cool stuff. Once it was all over and my Uber was transporting me back to my room at the Ritz Carlton, I asked him to stop so I could take a picture in front of the sign at Millennium Park. I didn't really go into the park, just to the corner, which was good enough for me.

18 ST. LOUIS

MISSOURI AUGUST 5, 2017

St. Louis, Missouri was the 18th stop on my 50-state adventure. I was hired by the company my new friend and partner, Adrian, worked for and we were on sort of a tour with some of the cast from the hit television series, Power. The crew was a part of special events that occurred in multiple cities throughout the country. What would happen is the local radio stations would give out free tickets to its listeners and people would be invited to these one night only, special events that consisted of a meet & greet, panel discussion, and brief concert showcase from some of the cast members. I was hired to create recap videos for the company to use for social media or internal use.

It was early August when I made it to Missouri, and I was confident in my first time visiting because not only was I not traveling alone, but also all of my accommodations were already taken care of by the company. This was not normally the case when I traveled; the majority of the time I traveled alone and paid for all my expenses. My girlfriend Tiffany would be on this trip with me, and it was always great to meet with Adrian on these special gigs. We were lodging at a very comfortable hotel and had lots of free time the day we arrived. Our first stop was to a restaurant not far from our hotel.

The food was great and very fulfilling. Later that day we went to see the St. Louis Arc, which is one of its famous landmarks. It was here that I decided to mark my next chapter in my journey. We had to move so far away from the Arc because it is so massive that it was hard to fit the full arc in picture, even with the camera standing horizontally. I sat down in the grass once we got far enough, and posed with the "peace sign", thankful to reach my 18th milestone, unharmed.

19 WICHITA
KANSAS SEPTEMBER 25, 2017

At the end of September, I began to realize how far of a distance I still had left to travel, and in comparison, to how many months had passed, I hadn't really made it that far. 75% of the year was gone and I hadn't even made it halfway. It was time to pick up the pace. Most of the states I visited by flying, and that system of traveling was pretty expensive. I figured I could either rent a vehicle or ask for a ride, so I called my cousin T. Reed. I offered him a percentage of anything I made while on the road, and I also gave him a generous per diem, which was a little lower than preferred, but I got the family discount. We cut out a few days to drive from Tulsa, Oklahoma straight up to Minot, North Dakota.

September 25th is when our expedition began. Our first stop was Wichita, Kansas where we met with iPhone Amari and Mackin Minnis. I was lucky enough to film these two videos while in Kansas. I found them through Instagram like almost all the artists I worked with, and I offered one a video for free and the other a video for as cheap as $100. It wasn't so much the money that I was interested in, it was more so the relationship and exposure. My game plan was as simple as getting my work in circulation in the city, then allow what I did for free to bring me back another time and I can charge full price.

When me and T. Reed arrived, we met iPhone Amari at a gas station. Kansas looked a lot like home and the people weren't noticeably different. iPhone Amari was a young and very energetic character and invited us to his friend's house to shoot. By the time we finished his music video I'd met 5 or 6 locals that did music or knew someone who did, including Mackin Minnis.

When we finished shooting, we got on the road and headed for Nebraska, but we didn't get very far before Mack called me and said he wanted to shoot. We gladly turned around, but before we got too far, we pulled into a parking garage to take a picture. It was raining outside and there weren't very many landmarks at my disposal, so I just posted up near a window. This day I marked my timeline for my 19th state, with only 3 months left to go.

20 OMAHA
NEBRASKA SEPTEMBER 26, 2017

Omaha, Nebraska was our second stop on our horizontal adventure. I didn't know what to expect upon arrival, but I was fairly prepared. I spoke with very many Omaha based artists months before my arrival, so I had plenty of shoots lined up for my arrival. I was lucky enough to film 2 videos while in Omaha, but I had more people who were supposed to film with me, but things happen. The first artists I worked with was Smoove, and my buddy Harry had made this shoot possible. Smoove was a very laid back individual, he was easy to work with and it didn't take us very long to do the shoot.

We did scenes in what people from Tulsa would likely refer to as the hood, and we also got more shots at a small burger joint in the city. Shortly after that we met with another Omaha artist by the name of Chikadibia. Chikadibia was full of stories and an animated character. He had colorful clothing on and a really big afro. We did the shoot in less than 30 minutes and it was all in front of a store, only a few offices down from the burger shack I was recently shooting at. Earlier that day immediately when I arrived in Omaha, I had already taken my picture to show the world where I was.

21 DES MOINES

IOWA SEPTEMBER 26, 2017

I was in Omaha, Nebraska when I decided I wanted to add a trip to Iowa. My cousin T. Reed was with me and we had just finished filming a video. A trip to Iowa was not originally a part of the plan. Our next stop was supposed to be Sioux Falls, South Dakota but after doing a little research on Google Maps, I realized that we weren't very far from Iowa.

I got on Instagram and began searching for hashtags that could help me find some potential artists to film with. It was already pretty late, but I was determined to find someone. This would make one less stop to make for the year. I was lucky enough to find an artist by the name of Rajan Monroe of Transparent Art Group. It was a blessing that he was ready to film even considering how late and spontaneous it was. It took us about 2 hours to get to Des Moines and when we arrived, we met at a local park and immediately began filming. After we finished, the guys were cool enough to fill up our gas tank and offered us a bite to eat.

Its wasn't much in comparison to what people initially pay for video services but the offer was accepted and very much appreciated. Optimism played a significant role on my 21st state because if it weren't for my being optimistic, add T. Reeds willingness to drive, I don't think I would have tried to visit the state. The trip was completely off the script, but it turned out to be great. 21 states later with barely 2 months left, and 29 states to go. I would have plenty more time to put my optimism to work.

22 SIOUX FALLS

SOUTH DAKOTA SEPTEMBER 27, 2017

The trip to South Dakota was not half bad considering the fact that T. Reed covered the majority of the driving. The first thing we did once we arrived was head for the nearest YMCA so we could clean up. YMCA's were golden because they provided shelter, showers, leisure activities and food was always nearby. Shortly after shooting hoops and showering, we went to meet our new Sioux Falls friends. Their names were Fayde and Yung AG. These guys were really charismatic and gave off a vibe that made me feel like they were from New York and LA.

When I heard the songs we would be shooting to, it made it obvious to me that these guys were a lot bigger than where they were coming from. We shot each of their videos then had a long debate on rather or not we would make the trip for North Dakota. After about 30 strong minutes of debating, we decided to go ahead and shoot back to Tulsa, and I would catch North Dakota some other time.

23 NEWARK
NEW JERSEY OCTOBER 20, 2017

I flew straight from Los Angeles to New Jersey the second I looked and saw that it would only cost me $178. I didn't spend more than 1 night there before I was back at the airport. I landed about 3PM and I would be flying out for Houston the next morning around 6aM. The second I made it to New Jersey I was trying to find a new artist by the name of Havek City.

We had managed to keep communication over the last year or so and it was such a surprise that I would be in the city and he was ready to work. The first place we went was to a barber shop so he could get freshened up then we headed out for some dope locations to catch some shots. We finished off in a nice hotel lobby and that's where I caught my Uber back to the airport to relax until it was time for my flight to take off. I could have hung around more, but I wasn't very sure of the area I was in and didn't plan on getting any surprises or taking any losses.

24 NEW YORK CITY
NEW YORK OCTOBER 22, 2017

For the majority of my travels, I booked one-way trips because I never knew when exactly I would need to leave. Two days prior to the 22nd of October I was in New Jersey, got a call from Adrian for a gig in Houston for the 23rd, and was back to the east coast the morning after that.

I didn't know what to expect when I got to New York. I've always seen movies that portrayed New York to be this place where people are packed shoulder-to-shoulder, always in a rush, and never using alley ways because you will get robbed. I made it to New York and had the complete opposite experience of what I expected. Although the traffic was pretty bad, it was bearable. The people have a real movie-like east coast accent, but the people weren't jam packed together. Everyone isn't on their phone and wearing suits and sunglasses, nor is everyone in a super rush, at least not where I was.

The first place I visited when I left the airport was Time Square. I didn't even stop to think that because it's such a popular place in New York, that it would be mostly occupied by tourists, like myself. Because it was such a popular attraction, I noticed all types of people. A large group of kids of Asian descent, a black couple that are speaking a language other than English, many different shades of skin, and different languages. It was just like Hollywood Blvd. in Los Angeles.

As I was standing on the sidewalk searching for a signal on my cell phone I accidently bumped into an elderly woman, maybe between the ages of 50-60 years old. It looked as if she were in the middle of her afternoon walk because of the sweat stains under her armpits and she was wearing a sun visor, fanny pack and curved-sole tennis shoes. But then again, I'd guess that most elderly tourist might choose that same attire. Well, we bumped shoulders and it was definitely accidental, so I quickly touched her arm and said, "excuse me", and she gave me a funky look and continued walking. I figured she gave me that ugly look because I'm black and I bumped into her, so in my mind I'm jokingly thinking that it doesn't matter how far you get from Oklahoma, racism will find you.

I shrugged it off and continued searching for a phone signal when out of nowhere I feel someone tapping my camera bag. I don't know anyone in New York, so I instantly think that it's a mugger trying to rob me, so I flex my jaw muscles, lower my eyebrows and dramatically turn around with this crazy look on my face. When I see who it is, I raise one brow and smirk the side of my lips because I can't believe who it is, or what's about to happen. I look down and see the same elderly woman that I just bumped into and I swear she's about to tell me I'd better watch myself. I pierce my dark brown eyes straight through her bright blue eyes as she adjusts her lips to speak.

This woman then says to me with the softest look on her face, "Thank you young man". So, I'm thinking to myself, what in the world is she thanking me for? She continues to say, "I have been walking around all morning and people have banged into me many times, but you are the first one to say excuse me. People here have been so rude, and I felt like I should tell you thank you for being kind." This blew my mind. She was right; people would bump into you and keep going like nothing happened.

It was at this moment the term "southern hospitality" popped into my head. Being told "thank you" is something you rarely hear for saying excuse me, at least in this fashion. I asked a black woman that seemed to be with her daughter if she could take a picture for me so that I could document my 24th achievement. The Big Apple was in the bag.

25 HARTFORD

CONNECTICUT OCTOBER 23, 2017

Early Monday morning, at about 5:30AM I boarded a bus for a 3-hour ride to Hartford, Connecticut. I wasn't very excited about going to Connecticut because I didn't exactly have anyone to work with. I was determined to find someone by the time I got there, but I didn't have anyone when I boarded my bus. I spent about an hour reaching out to as many artists in the area that I could find, and eventually I was able to find a producer that was excited to let me film him putting together a beat. It was a stretch but, anything would work. When I look back on my trip, I wish I did a better job of preparing. If I would have done a little better of a job with preparing, my trip could have been 100x more lucrative and a lot less stressful.

When the bus stopped, I immediately had an Uber drop me off at the address he told me, and we met at a Little Caesar's pizza. The producer I had the honor of working with in Connecticut went by the name of Matrix Man, but as a producer he preferred the name Bendin Beats. He was a cool, hippie like character and welcomed me into his home with open arms. I didn't waste much time getting the filming done, considering the fact that I had another bus to catch after I finished filming for him. All we ended up doing was vibing for about an hour and listening to some beats while I recorded. Soon after I was back on my way to the bus station.

26 BOSTON

MASSACHUSETTS OCTOBER 24, 2017

My bus arrived in Boston early Tuesday morning. The previous night was a really long wait, waiting for 9AM to come so I could ride to Boston. When I arrived, I caught an Uber from the station to an Airbnb I had rented for the night. This was my first time ever purchasing an Airbnb for myself. I had stayed the night in plenty over the years, but none of them were ever my own. My experience with this Airbnb was unlike any that I had stayed at up to that date. It was a little less than $100 but that wasn't nearly as high as the hotel prices were. When I arrived at the Airbnb, checking in wasn't hard at all, but the only thing that startled me was about 1 hour into my stay I heard moving around, I later found out that it was a shared location that had 3 rooms being rented out at once.

It made me uneasy about leaving my belongings at the Airbnb because I didn't want to risk coming so far to potentially take a loss. When I think back on it now, I feel like I was being extremely overprotective, but better safe than sorry, right? It was near evening time when I was picked up by the artist I would be filming for the evening, Jay Mosa, his uncles and photographer. We stacked up inside their vehicle and went to a nearby Barnes and Noble. It was here that we filmed the majority of our music video, then left and got the last shots at some areas around the area nearby. I wish I had it in the budget to go do more enjoyable things with my free time after shoots but, every dollar was vitally important in making sure I made it back home.

27 SEABROOK
NEW HAMPSHIRE OCTOBER 24, 2017

At the end of my shoot with Mosa, I told him I could hook him up with a free video if he did himself and me a huge favor. He was excited to get a new video, so I was also excited to make my proposal. I told him that I would shoot him an additional video if he would be willing to catch at least one of the scenes to the video in New Hampshire. It sounded crazy at first, but when here realized we were only a 30-minute drive from the closest city of New Hampshire to Massachusetts he was instantly on board. Seabrook, New Hampshire is where we took our production of the evening.

I didn't experience much of Seabrook because it was dark and we were only passing through, but I did notice that the homes were built high above the ground. I'm assuming this was because the city was so close to the ocean that the water was likely to rise pretty high in the area we passed through. We pulled over on the side of the road next to a shack on the ocean side and got a few shots and headed back to Boston. It was a quick and easy shoot, and I was happy I could pull things together to make that work out because lord knows it would be a slim chance that I ever come back to New Hampshire had I not had a successful attempt during that trip.

28 PORTLAND

MAINE OCTOBER 25, 2017

After a long bus ride from Boston Massachusetts I finally arrived In Portland, Maine. This is the furthest I have ever been away from home, while still being in the United States. I can't think of any reason a person from my hood would ever have been to Maine, other than to intentionally visit every state in the country. I didn't know what to expect when I got to Maine, but I sure did not expect to see any black people.

By the grace of God, the first people to respond to me, were black. Being so far away from home, it just made me feel more comfortable to be around people of a similar race. I made it to the city or Portland and the new friends I was working with went by the name of Quarter Pound. They were all really cool people and I can't wait to get back and visit them again. We shot the video at random areas around the city then they took me to grab a bite to eat. Once it was all over, they dropped me off at my hotel and I rested up in preparation for my next destination.

29 BURLINGTON

VERMONT OCTOBER 26, 2017

The last bus I caught while in New England was to Burlington, Vermont. The bus rides were comfortable on the overnight trips because there were less people. When I would wake from my naps on the bus it was relaxing just staring out of the window, studying the different views and city architectures. I caught an Uber straight to a nice cheap hotel when I arrived in Burlington. It was late when I arrived so most of the hotel's rooms were already occupied.

The woman at the check in counter made a mistake and gave me the key to a room that was already occupied, so I was very surprised when I walked into the room to see that the sheets were already pulled over, shoes were in the floor, and food was on the counter. Lucky for me there wasn't anyone in the room that I would have awkwardly walked in on, and lucky for them I'm not a thief.

I was only at the hotel long enough to set my things down and set up my laptop before my new friend Colby picked me up from the hotel and took me to the venue we would be shooting at. It was a really chill environment and although shooting the video had its good vibes, I truly just enjoyed hanging out with the fellas I was shooting the video for. I didn't spend very much time in the city other than that night, and I left the next morning.

30 BIRMINGHAM
ALABAMA OCTOBER 27, 2017

Alabama was amongst the simplest trips of all 47 states. I flew into Birmingham, Alabama from Burlington, Vermont and went directly to the Magic City Classic. This was my first time ever in Alabama other than passing through. I didn't see much of the city, but it did remind me of Oklahoma. I was filming a recap video for AT&T while there, but I didn't get a chance to see the game. There was a lot of people at the Magic City classic and it was really cold that day.

After I finished shooting, I went back to check in to my room at the Redmont Hotel Downtown Birmingham. It was a nice hotel and when I was there, I met with a good friend from Tulsa name Boss P. He was a really supportive character and he had just so happened to be a few minutes away in a nearby city. We met up at the hotel and put a short music video together before I went back to my room to call it a night.

31 PHILADELPHIA

PENNSYLVANIA NOVEMBER 15, 2017

My trip to Philly was fast. I was picked up from the airport by the artist I was shooting a video for. He was a cool character by the name of Poe Coliyon. He was just like a lot of the other artists I was filming for, surprised that I actually showed up. We made the shoot simple and then he returned me to the airport so that I could fly to my next state.

32 BALTIMORE

MARYLAND NOVEMBER 17, 2017

The week I arrived in Baltimore, Maryland was a part of a very busy week. Just two days prior I was in Philadelphia, Pennsylvania. I flew from Philly to Vegas for one day, then right back to the east coast where I landed in Washington DC. I landed around midnight, entering into Friday, November 17th. I booked a room on hotwire so I would have a place to lodge for the night. I booked through Hotwire's Hot Rates options so I didn't know exactly what hotel I would be in before paying, but I did know what area I would be in, and that was just about all that mattered. I was lucky enough to get a Hilton, just outside of DC, in Sterling, Virginia. I woke up early Friday morning to go to the Union Station so that I could catch the bus to Baltimore.

When I finally made it to Baltimore it was still early in the day, about 12PM I had been keeping contact with a very popular Baltimore artist by the name of President Davo. Months ago, I had reached out to him on Instagram, not really expecting him to reply, but he did. We arranged a shoot and I finally showed up to Baltimore to follow through on my promise. I had no clue what to expect and I was very uncomfortable when I arrived because he wasn't at the address he gave me. I didn't want to get out of the Uber until I was sure of where to go, so I hung around for a second or two. But then the Uber driver began to look irritated, so I let him go.

Davo finally hit me back and told me that I was at the right place, I just needed to come to the back of the building. I was uncomfortable, but I was never scared. I'm on unfamiliar grounds, dealing with people I don't know, doing things I wouldn't recommend to my best of friends, but I always figured this, "I have come too far to let my plans change". I meet Davo at the back of the building I was parked at for so long and when I see him, I feel accomplished.

He introduced me to a bunch of his friends, and to the featured artist that was on the song we filmed, TateKo Bang. These guys are very popular. I didn't know it then, but I would soon find out. We didn't waste any time getting started and I enjoyed the time I spent filming with The System, which was the name of their crew. I was filming this project for free, but Davo paid me anyways and I noted that about him. As we were wrapping up the shoot, I realized it was time to post another milestone for the world to see. I asked Davo to hop in the shot with me and one of his friends took the picture. State number 32 was in the books, and this added another notch in my confidence of meeting my goal.

33 ALEXANDRIA
VIRGINIA NOVEMBER 18, 2017

My trip to Virginia was one of the most similar to my trip to New Hampshire. My hotel was in Sterling, Virginia, but the artists that I was shooting for stayed in Washington D.C. I ended up catching an Uber from my hotel in Virginia to them in D.C. where we caught our first few shots but part of the deal was, I would shoot their video free of charge if only they would agree to shoot a portion of the video in Virginia. They confirmed to the terms so for our last shot we went just over the bridge to Alexandria Virginia. The area was decorated with holiday lights and had a river running right along the side of the area we were in. There, we got the last few shots of our music video and they dropped me off at the D.C. bus terminal.

34 WILMINGTON
DELAWARE NOVEMBER 18, 2017

Delaware was far from what I expected. My idea of Delaware before I arrived was honestly that it would be full of eastern coast country folk and lots of river docks around. When I got off of the bus that dropped me off in Wilmington I was in for a rude awakening. My first stop when I arrived was to a shopping district to purchase some shoes. It didn't take long for me to realize that Wilmington, Delaware was a predominately black city.

I stopped by a shoe store and found a bunch of Air Jordan Retro's at a steal price. I bought 2 pair of shoes and went to the nearest post office to ship them to my home address. considering I wouldn't be home for quite some time and I didn't have the space to carry two large boxes of shoes around the country with me.

It was at this post office in Wilmington, Delaware that I met the artists that I would be shooting a video for. They were two young high schoolers that I had met through a reference off of Instagram. We walked around the city to a few different places where we caught the shots for our video then they showed me to a corner convenience store that had some really good fried chicken. After the shoot I caught an Uber to the nearby New York City airport where I would be flying out to Alabama.

35 ORLANDO
FLORIDA NOVEMBER 18, 2017

My trip to Orlando Florida was a spur of the moment decision. I was ready to leave Wilmington, Delaware and was deciding how I would get home (by bus, rental, airplane). I started clicking around on the net and was blown away when I found a last- minute trip to Orlando, Florida for only 76.20. I caught an Uber from Wilmington, Delaware over to the Philadelphia Airport and was on my way. My ride from Delaware to Philly was actually really short and the only thing that made it comparatively long was the traffic.

The whole ride to the airport I was on Instagram notifying every person I had ever talked to from Florida that I was on my way and my stay would be short! When I arrived in Orlando after my 3-hour flight from Philly, I was happy to find out that my new friends Aris and Tony of music group Onajidox were already at the airport waiting on me. I jumped straight in with them and we conversed the whole way on our short drive to the mall.

We knew it would be a possibility that the mall security would ask us to leave but it was a risk well worth taking since we did have much time. Luckily, we were able to get all of our shots without any issues. It was until we were passing the Florida Hotel, which was connected to the mall, that I realized the perfect place to take a picture that would best illustrate my location. I took a picture in front of the Florida hotel marquee and posted it on my social media platforms for everyone to see. 15 states to go, 2 months to do it.

36 LEESVILLE

LOUISIANA DECEMBER 9, 2017

December 9th marked the first day of what would be a super adventure. For the next week or so, I would be making a huge trip around the country in order to get my goal done. The first stop was Leesville, Louisiana. To get there from Tulsa, Oklahoma I passed through Texas. Just as I was about to enter Texas while passing thorough a small town called Hugo, I was pulled over by a patrol officer. I wasn't surprised that he pulled me over because when I noticed him on the opposite side of the road going the opposite direction, I instantly looked down at my speedometer.

It said 85mph and I was in a 70, looked in my rear view mirror and I just so happened to be speeding past a state trooper at the same place where he could easily make a U-turn between the medians. He gave me a $375 ticket that would later turn into a warrant, but I didn't let it throw me off of my mission. I did the speed limit the rest of the way to Leesville, and completely forgot about my experience with the officer by the time I made it there.

Leesville is a small town, but I enjoyed my time there. The people were easy going, and lots of black folk occupied the town. I didn't feel unsafe or threatened at any point of my visit. I met with my guy Yngin and it didn't take us much of anytime to get our video finished. We were at a cul-de-sac at the end of his street when I noticed a water tower that had "Leesville" printed on it in large letters. It was obvious to me that I wouldn't find a much better place to illustrate where I was, so I had him take a few pictures of me posing in front the water tower.

37 JACKSON
MISSISSIPPI DECEMBER 10, 2017

I drove to many states at the end of the year in hopes of completing my 50-state goal. I'm sure Mississippi has much to offer but due to last minute circumstances, Jackson, Mississippi, became my least favorite stop on my 12-month trip. Before my arrival I had scheduled shoots with 3 difference local artists. None of them showed. I was flaked on and it was a horrible feeling. I drove 10+ hours to arrive in Jackson and had no reward for it. I contacted as many artists as I could and eventually made contact with one. But unfortunately, he wouldn't be ready until the following day.

Nothing ended up working out, so I decided to make a montage video that illustrated Downtown Jackson, and then I moved on to the next state. Just before I took off, I decided that I would still document my location with a picture, even though I didn't do a video for any specific person. If didn't feel good but I moved on to the next stop with my head up, but I never thought I would have been flaked on.

38 CHARLESTON

SOUTH CAROLINA DECEMBER 10, 2017

The third stop of my adventure led me to Charleston, South Carolina. Charleston was a significant stop for 2 reasons. One was because I understood that history says this was the city where the first African slave entered the country. The second reason this city was significant to me was because I had recently finished reading Charlemagne tha God's book called "Black Privilege" and he spoke about spending a lot of his earlier years in this city. My time in Charleston was very short; I was only there for a matter of hours. Maybe only 2 hours.

I met with an artist by the name of Twaun and he had a strong accent. I never understood how people so close to the eastern border could have a stronger southern accent than actual southern folk, but it is definitely possible. Twaun was a really respectful and relaxed individual. We shot at a few areas around the city and then he gave me a bunch of free merch before I went on my way. It was as we were walking down the street that I noticed the Charleston Music Hall and figured this would be a good place to take a picture for my followers to see. Soon after that, I was back on the road in route to my next destination.

39 CHARLOTTE
NORTH CAROLINA DECEMBER 11, 2017

During this week of my United States adventure, I spent the majority of my days driving, and the nighttime sleeping, or filming. I tried to reserve as much of my money for food and gas, so I didn't get a hotel any of these nights. I would stop at YMCA's to shower, if I did shower, but I was so focused on getting back to Tulsa that I didn't spend any time wasting time. Some nights I would get so tired that I would just pull over into gas station parking lots and pass out.

The night I arrived in North Carolina I met with artist Teezy Montana and like every other night, we got right to work. Teezy was cool, and he blessed me with some of his merch before we finished shooting. We went downtown to get some drone shots and the last of our performance shots. It was freezing outside, and I didn't have more than my thin leather jacket that night, but we made it happen.

40 MORGANTOWN
WEST VIRGINIA DECEMBER 11, 2017

West Virginia was an interesting trip. The drive there was fun because there were lots of mountains and overpasses that kept me engaged during the ride. I went straight to West Virginia University where I would meet the artist I was shooting for. His name was Johnny Bonez and he was a student at the school. It was our first time meeting in person, and he allowed me to use his shower before we hit the road to the place where we would be shooting our first scene.

It was in a rural area in the middle of nowhere. We walked into the woods and beyond to an area that a river once passed through. After we finished filming there, we made our way for Charleston, West Virginia. I enjoyed this area because it reminded me of home. I didn't spend very much time in Charleston after we arrived, so we got our shots and went to a mall and left from there.

41 LOUISVILLE

KENTUCKY DECEMBER 12, 2017

Louisville, Kentucky was the 6th stop on my 10-state field trip, at the end of the year. It was late when I arrived in Kentucky, but I met my new friend Ralo at a skate park in the city and we got right to work. Ralo was a humble and energetic character. We finished the shoot in about 1 hour and used the downtown skate park as our only location.

After I finished shooting for him, I headed to my next shoot not far away from where I already was, to shoot for another artist by the name of Otto Black. Otto was happy to see me and excited that I followed through on my word of coming. My shoot with Bruce was just as fast as the last one was. I didn't do much in Kentucky but the time I did spend there with the artists was enjoyable.

42 IDIANAPOLIS
INDIANA DECEMBER 12, 2017

Indianapolis was a special visit for me because I had made connections with someone named Big City who was good friends with a popular radio personality from Tulsa. His name was Feeray and I had been in contact with him months in advance. Unfortunately, I would not be able to meet with him on this trip, but he was able to link me in with a very good artist. The artist's name was J. Stokes and he was a very laid back individual.

I probably sat in an empty parking lot for about 4 hours before I finally got in touch with him, but it was early when I arrived so I couldn't complain. I met J. Stokes at his house when I arrived and followed him to a few different locations from there. Indiana was similar to Oklahoma in architecture. We were walking across a small field when I took my picture.

43 MILWAUKEE

WISCONSIN DECEMBER 12, 2017

I drove directly from Indianapolis to Milwaukee after my shoot with J. Stokes. I remember all the drives were long and it was mostly nighttime when I would commute between states. I listened to a lot of Nipsey Hussle's music, Nephew Tommy prank calls on YouTube, and ET the HipHop Preacher's mixtapes were on repeat. I would make a lot of stops at convenience stores that I would pass just so that I could get out of the car and stretch my legs.

There was one specific drink I owe a tremendous amount of my success of getting state to state to, and that is Sprite. I would buy 2 or 3 Sprites between each state and about 2 bags of Jolly Ranchers per bottle. I would stuff as many of the Jolly Ranchers into a half filled bottle of Sprite as I could fit and let it sit in the dashboard for a day or so, that way the hard candy could melt inside the drink. It would make for a really sweet, syrup-like substance that I would drink, and it kept my energy high and made me super attentive.

The sun was down by the time I arrived in Milwaukee, but it wasn't very late. I met with my new friends, Nate Brady and CY, and we all took a short ride to the Downtown area. Our shoot was quick and easy, so after we finished, I drove to Minneapolis and found a good spot to catch some z's. I was always cautious of falling asleep with the car running because I thought I heard that you could die from inhaling a bunch of something. But it was so cold outside I figured I was doomed if I did and doomed if I didn't so I took my chances. Carbon Monoxide poisoning! That's what it's called.

44 MINOT

NORTH DAKOTA DECEMBER 13, 2017

Minot, North Dakota was the 9th stop on my 10-state field trip. The drive from Milwaukee to Minot was 12+ hours in total but since I stopped to get rest in Minneapolis, the drive was cut in half. By the time I arrived in Minot it was about 5pm and the sun was already going down. I went straight to the home of the artists I would be filming for, Tru. He lived in a nice home off the side of a highway and when I made it there, he was happy to see that I actually came. I didn't spend very much time in Minot outside of the time spent shooting because I was ready to get back to Tulsa. We went downtown and got some shots inside of a random parking garage then we wrapped up the shoot. Tru was a cool person and he bragged to me about how he would be moving to Atlanta soon.

45 CASPER
WYOMING DECEMBER 14, 2017

On December 14th I arrived in Casper, Wyoming from Minot, North Dakota. As I drove through the state, I really appreciated the landscape views of the open plains for grass and large scattered rocks, as if someone just removed some mountains and left over some huge boulders. I went directly to a YMCA in the town to shower and change clothes, and after I finished, I played basketball while I anticipated replies from a few artists I had reached out to that lived in the area. It didn't take long before I had a shoot booked.

The artist, David of a rock band by the name of the Residential Fuck Ups. He met me at the YMCA and I followed him around the corner to his house that he was room mating with another friend of his. We shot the music video right in his garage and it turned out really good. We went back around the corner to the YMCA where he dropped me off and saw some Antelope crossing the street.

This was a mind blowing experience to me because at home in Tulsa, Oklahoma the deer and antelope are usually spotted running across the street or on the sides of the highway. The Antelope in Casper were fearlessly walking in the streets with no worry of being hit by the stopped traffic. They were almost like stray dogs just wandering around, which is unheard of in Tulsa when it comes to wildlife like deer and antelope.

46 HONOLULU

HAWAII DECEMBER 22, 2017

It was a few days before Christmas when I began my trip to Honolulu, Hawaii. I wasn't very sure I would finish the remainder of the states at this part of the year because there were only so many days left, it was costly to travel, and I was honestly beginning to get tired. I took the last of my money to book a one-way trip to Hawaii, which I would only be there for about 5 hours, and from there I would be headed to Alaska. This cost me a little over $600 in flights just getting to Honolulu. I decided the best thing I could do was fly to LA and hang out there for a couple days and try to scrape up a few dollars, then take my talents straight across the water from there.

My thought process was simple, I didn't have enough in the budget to get hotels and romance the trip, so my stops were a few hours per city, then get back home. On top of all the traveling I was paying for, I had to remember that I had a regular life and monthly bills that still needed its share of my profits. I had my goal in mind so decision making was a lot easier than it would have been had I not known what I wanted. But nonetheless, there were some stressful times. The flight to Hawaii was graceful. I don't remember it being any turbulence on the flight over and we soared above the clouds the whole trip. When it was time to land, the sun sat right over the ocean and it was the true definition of beautiful.

The colors in the sky reflected over the ocean, the only thing that could have made it better would be for a mermaid to flip out of the water. When people ask, I always tell them that Hawaii was my favorite stop of the whole trip. It was 3 days before Christmas, but it felt like the middle of spring in Honolulu. Los Angeles has nice weather, but not this nice. The people were everything that the movies make them out to be. Samoan and humble. I met some of the coolest people ever.

The first thing I did when I arrived was meet with my new friend Joel. He was and is a really dope artist and had one of the coolest music videos I had ever seen while on my trip. We met at a mall where he introduced me to a few of his friends and then we went to get a bite to eat. I forget the name of the food I tried, but it was basically raw fish. It wasn't sushi or any of the regular raw foods you hear people eat here on the mainland, but it was a block of red raw fish. It was terrible. But I ate it. He introduced me to my first bite of tofu it was similar in taste to the other foods I ate. Not the most desirable. Later we started to head into the mountains, but I told him that I only had a few more hours left on the island and I wouldn't be able to accompany him. He understood and we blessed each other and parted ways.

Shortly thereafter I met with my other new friend Labrone Jr. He drove me around the city and introduced me to another artist who was interested in shooting a video with me. We finally went to a basketball court where we shot the music video and then played some pickup with the guys who were out there. I really enjoyed the time I spent in Honolulu and I can't wait to go back just to look at the city, be around the kind people, and feel that sweet breeze again.

47 FAIRBANKS

ALASKA DECEMBER 23, 2017

I arrived in Anchorage at about 7AM after a late night take off from Honolulu at 11PM. It was a 6-hour flight from one state to the other and that was the longest nonstop domestic flight I had ever taken in my life. Thankfully, I had plenty of exercise the night before, so I'm happy to say I slept the majority of the trip.

By the time I landed in Anchorage I had plenty of time to talk with a friend I had networked a connection with from my Oregon trip. While in Portland/Eugene Oregon working with Ab$oloot, he had a collaborative project he did long distance with Starbucks of Fairbanks, Alaska. They had previously done a song together and decided that I would shoot the scenes for Loot in Oregon, and a videographer by the name of Crimeski would shoot the scenes for Bucks in Anchorage. I didn't know at the time, but I soon found out that this ended up working out greatly in my favor.

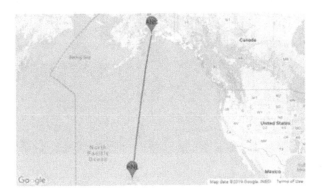

Flight	Departs	Arrives	Class	Traveler(s)	Seat(s)
~~Alaska~~	Honolulu (HNL)	Anchorage (ANC)	K	Jayon Mckinney	28B
Alaska 871	Fri, Dec 22	Sat, Dec 23	(Coach)		
Boeing 737-800	11:45 pm	7:15 am			

Starbucks and I came to the agreement that he would purchase my flight from Anchorage to Fairbanks and have me back to Anchorage in time to make my return flight to the mainland. I sat at the airport for about 2 or 3 hours before my flight from Anchorage to Fairbanks took off, so I used that time to edit Rebel Yelln's video that I had shot the night before.

By the time I landed in Fairbanks I was in for an obvious, but rude awakening. It was freezing outside. All I had was a thin Tulsa Progression hoodie and that to -4° weather was complete suicide. Starbucks could not help but laugh but thankfully he was prepared for the worst and got me a heavy Carhartt jacket.

We didn't have very much time to waste so we got right to work. Midway through our shoot we were at the University of Alaska Fairbanks and I decided that that was the area I wanted to make my 47-state statement. I wanted to be somewhere that had a fair representation of where I was, so we went in front of the information board. It was freezing so we made it quick. I put my hands inside of my jacket's pockets, opened my arms wide, and put my head down to block as much of the breeze as I could. Today I made it to 47 of the United States in less than a year.

Later that evening we grabbed burgers at Friar Tucks then headed to the airport. Thankfully, when I landed in Anchorage, Crimeski was already there to pick me up. This was our first time meeting in person and I'm sure he didn't know what to expect. Most of the people I met over the course of 2017 were surprised that I was actually there. The goal was unbelievable to hear about but even more unbelievable to witness. Crimeski was quiet for the most part at first, probably waiting for me to hit him over the head with a rock and begin harvesting his organs, but by the time we arrived at our first location I think he realized that wouldn't be happening.

Crimeski was to his city of Anchorage, what I was to the city of Tulsa. He was the guy you call when you need any kind of dope music videos or promo videos done. He is the closest you could get to a Cole Bennett or Azae Productions without having to spend the thousands of dollars. Anyways, Crimeski agreed to set me up with a shoot when I arrived in the city. I told him I would pay him for helping me out, but he turned down my offer and agreed to do it for free as long as he got producer credits on the project. He introduced me to the Trill Twins, made up by Jay Reeder and Loner Luc. These were a couple of the coolest stoner black guys I had ever met. They had the swag of someone you would meet in LA, cracking jokes, lots of jokes and smoking weed. Really easy going. They were happy to shoot so we got right to work.

47/50